Leader Guide

CHAINED
no
MORE

A Journey Of Healing For Adult Children Of Divorce

Robyn Besemann

Edited by Stephanie McIver
Cover Design by David Choates

This curriculum is not intended to be used as a replacement for therapists, counselors, or other healthcare professionals. It is designed to be an additional resource to assist in the healing process of participants. If further help is needed, please refer individuals to a psychologist or healthcare professional.

For more information, contact:
Robyn Besemann
E-mail address: *robyn@robynbministries.com*
Web address: *robynbministries.com*

WestBow Press books may be ordered through booksellers or by contacting:

WestBow Press
A Division of Thomas Nelson
1663 Liberty Drive
Bloomington, IN 47403
www.westbowpress.com
1-(866) 928-1240

ISBN: 978-1-4497-5390-0 (sc)
ISBN: 978-1-4497-5389-4 (e)

Library of Congress Control Number: 2012909534

Printed in the United States of America

WestBow Press rev. date: 07/25/2012

LETTER TO LEADERS

You have a magnificent opportunity to be used by the Lord to touch the lives of those adults who have lived with the pain of the divorce of their parents, whether they experienced it as young children, teens, or adults.

The pain and damage of a parent's divorce includes issues of trust, abandonment, betrayal, loyalty, loneliness, etc. The older a person gets, the easier it is to put the pain aside and just "live life." What happens many times, however, is that those issues arise again and again throughout life and negatively affect many areas of a person's life.

The purpose of *Chained No More* is to help adults look back at the divorce of their parents, face their hurt, see the power it continues to have on their lives to this point, heal from it, release it, and then learn practical tools to move forward in strength toward healthier choices and a brighter future.

Many times, kids of divorce experience what is described as the "sleeper effect." They seem to be fine and adjust to the divorce of their parents when it happens—they do fine in school and seem to accept what has happened—but when they get to their twenties, issues seem to creep in as they begin to look at serious relationships and possible marriage. All of a sudden, they find they have difficulty trusting others or become afraid to be alone. They may become overly possessive of people they love or find they don't trust people or their word. Maybe they lose their temper on a regular basis and turn to verbal or physical abuse. Many young adults discover that they don't have an interest in God at all, don't understand loyalty, find it impossible to make a long-term commitment, and find it difficult to fit in with others.

When issues arise around weddings, funerals, celebrations, or other family events, the loyalty issues become magnified and the tension continues. If there are multiple step-family members, the issues multiply.

Also, the older a child of divorce gets, the more he or she experiences divorce himself or herself with friends, other family members, and people in our society. The media is full of stories of broken families; even comedy shows try to make us laugh about the tragedy of divorce. Divorce just isn't funny!

Divorce rates in our world are at all-time highs, and it seems that divorce is just another option for personal happiness. How sad that marriage has evolved into almost an optional and temporary activity in life.

If we realized that our wedding vows were made to God first and our spouse second, it could make a difference in our resolve to do all we can to be committed for a long and healthy lifetime marriage, as God intended.

Whether you, as a leader have been divorced or not, are a child of your parents' divorce, or have seen friends or family members experience this tragedy, know that God is the Healer and will give you the wisdom and guidance to bring attendees of *Chained No More* toward His healing.

May God bless you as you serve Him by serving others!

LEADER REQUIREMENTS

This curriculum is based on the Word of God—the Bible. Scripture verses are taken from the NIV translation of the Bible unless otherwise noted.

<u>To be consistent with the basis of the Bible, all leaders must:</u>

- be born-again believers who are living a close walk with God;

- attend a Bible-believing church on a regular basis;

- have the permission and blessing of the senior pastor of that church;

- be above reproach in the way they live their life;

- understand that ministering to the hurting can present awkward situations, so the leader must be wise and use great discretion when ministering to someone of the opposite gender, choosing the location of ministering, etc. and

- be willing to spend an adequate amount of time preparing for and praying over each session.

FACILITATING A "CHAINED NO MORE" GROUP

Thank you for investing in *Chained No More*. This curriculum was developed because of the hurt seen in the children and teens experiencing divorce as well as the long-term damage in adults in their relationships, decisions, and ways they try to cope with the pain they try to hide or ignore.

CHAINED NO MORE GOALS:

1. To help participants look back at the experience of their parents' divorce and recognize the power it has had over their lives
2. To help participants express and accept the grief and then explore the areas in their lives that have been affected
3. To walk participants toward God's healing and help develop a closer relationship with Him
4. To give practical tools for stronger relationships and better decision-making based on healthy thinking, not past hurts

SUGGESTIONS:

- Each class should last one and a half to two hours. Please allow time for discussions.
- A meal may be included; however, to cover all the material, you should plan on at least two hours for the entire class if serving a meal.
- This curriculum is flexible, because every group will be different, have different dynamics, and have a variety of people of various ages, personalities, and levels of hurt. Become a student of each participant and ask the Lord for clear guidance as a leader.

FACILITATOR ADVICE:

- It is important to make sure the group understands that everything said in the room is confidential. Nothing should be shared or discussed about anyone in the class outside of the group.
- You will need to let participants know that leaders will be discussing the group after every session so all leaders are on the same page. This debrief helps you to be more effective as a team. Leaders will not share with anyone else.
- Let participants know that all of the leaders will be lifting each group member up in prayer throughout the week. Encourage your leaders to be faithful in that.
- You must understand how frightening and intimidating a class such as this can be to first-time group members. They are going to share their personal hurts and fears and trust you with that information. They trust that you will not preach to them, be judgmental of them, or gossip about what is shared.
- Participants may bring up something that they have never remembered or shared before. It may surprise them. Let them "chew" on it for a moment and share what they can. There is nothing wrong with some silence as they process, cry or whatever. A good question after a minute or two is, "So, what are you thinking?" Some of what might come up can be very frightening to them. There is a difference between prying for information and guiding someone to think deeper. If they are unable to continue, please respect that and move on. You might be able to connect with them later. Please let participants know from the very first class that if there is something you don't understand or know how to do, you will be going to one of your resources for advice so you can minister well. Let them know that you will not be sharing their name. It might be good to also let them know, that if they

have a therapist/counselor at this time, they might go to them if things get too rough (flashbacks, anxiety attacks, etc.) for some additional help,

- Please advise them not to go into detail with family members about what is going on in *Chained No More* during the three months they are in class. The reason for that is because their family may discount what they say, make them feel guilty or a dysfunctional family may bring them down and keep them from healing. The point of this program is to "break the chains". It is not to isolate family members, but to allow for healing.

- The healing in *Chained No More* comes from the Holy Spirit through the questions they answer in their books. The Lord reveals things, so you do not need to lecture or fill all the spaces with talking. There is plenty of room for them to sit quietly, reflect and fill out their pages.

- To preserve the confidentiality and safety of the class, it is important that there not be visitors in this class or any new participants after the first or second week.

- Feel free to share some things about yourself, but don't monopolize the time and don't make it so heavy that they feel they need to help YOU or can't trust that you have lived what you are leading. On the other hand, if you share only the good things about yourself and your life, it can make it look like you are superior to them and that is not healthy either. Be real, but use good discretion.

- DO NOT let the participants take their books home until after the last class. The reason for this is because most of them will look ahead and that can water down what they just went through or were made aware of. Also, family members may look at their book and cause more chaos. Please buy a tub and put the books in it after each class and promise them that no one will be looking at the books between classes. Please never look into the books. Participants must be able to trust your word.

- Please arrive early enough to have the room completely set up when participants arrive. It is better to calmly welcome them and not be rushing around setting up when they arrive.

- Have only water available to hydrate their brains; not tea or coffee or soda. Snacks are appropriate if you feel you have time. Sometimes a little social time in the middle of a session helps participants relax.

- There are a lot of Scripture verses in this curriculum as we show them Truth. Please don't add more and more, but let the Lord bring His truths through the pages. Please stay away from subjects that can cause division and distract from the base purpose.

- You may have participants who are not Christians; even some who are agnostics or atheists. Let them know that you are not going to "beat them over the head with a Bible" and that you will respect their beliefs, however, this curriculum is based on the Bible and you believe the Bible is the Word of God.

- You may sense some hesitation from someone to share something about their parents because they may feel like they are disrespecting them or being disloyal; especially if their parents have passed away or are ill. Please assure them again that the intent of this class is not to do that. It is only to see how their childhood may have affected their lives in negative ways and to heal from them. Remind them that their parents had their own hurts and they weren't born to hurt people. It was the chains they carried too. Hopefully, there will be understanding, grace and eventually, forgiveness given to their parents.

- Let participants know that their family members and friends may not know how to respond to them as participants heal and change their way of thinking and acting. Participants may come back and tell you about how their relationships are changing. Encourage them to be patient, stay in prayer about it and focus on their own personal healing right now. They will be setting up healthier boundaries, but must do it with grace and the love they have for people in their lives.

- An effective place to open each session with prayer is directly after going through the "session goals" with the class.

- Be creative in encouraging group members throughout the week. *Chained No More* leaders are not therapists with a couch and an hour. Let the Holy Spirit guide you in this, and be faithful in His leading. Decide how you will make up a missed session by a participant.

- This Leader Guide will give you many tools to use for healing in the group. Be creative, and be sensitive to the Lord's leading in implementing the activities each week.

- Please keep the chapters in order as written so healing can be most effective.

Please go to the Robyn B Ministries website (www.robynbministries.com) to the store page and download Home Links. Copy and give to participants to take home each week.

If you have questions, concerns, or suggestions, please contact Robyn at *robyn@robynbministries.com*.

TABLE OF CONTENTS

SAFETY AND RESPECT GUIDELINES

To make this class successful, it is important to feel safe to share thoughts, opinions, and feelings so we can heal and move toward a better future. Confidentiality is of utmost importance.

PLEASE READ THESE GUIDELINES TO YOUR CLASS AND FOLLOW THEM:

- This is a SAFETY ZONE. What is said in this class stays here. Please refrain from talking about what is shared in class to others outside of the class or group.

- Show respect for one another by
  - not interrupting;
  - accepting the participants for who they are, where they are, and what they have gone through; and
  - refraining from using vulgar or offensive language.

- Everyone's opinions and answers are important.

- There are no wrong answers or feelings.

- Everyone should have an opportunity to speak and be heard.

LINKS IN YOUR CHAIN
(Part One)

IDENTIFYING

SESSION ONE
Links In Your Chain (Part One)
Beginning The Journey

Welcome to the first week of *Chained No More!* The most important part of session one is to begin to build trust in the group. Everyone should feel safe to share their feelings without fear of judgment.

 ## SESSION GOALS

- Begin to get to know one another
- Begin to build trust in leaders and group members
- Learn about the purpose of *Chained No More* and how you can benefit the most from it
- Understand the Safety and Respect Guidelines so you can feel safe and valued
- Identify and acknowledge the issues that may have been caused by the divorce of your parents

GROUP GAB

1. Welcome group members, and thank them for coming.
2. Have participants introduce themselves to each other.
3. Introduce your leaders, and have them share why they wanted to be part of this group.
4. Ask participants to share their *fears* and *hopes* for this class, and write them on a board.
5. Remind participants that things shared in this group will not be discussed outside of the class; however, group leaders will debrief as a team after each session so they are ministering in unity.
6. Go over safety and respect guidelines
7. Have participants read "Just for You" and the following verse on page 2.
8. Have group fill out "The Chains in Your Story" (page vi) and then collect them.

TELL YOUR STORY

Give each person a chance to tell his or her story in ten minutes, beginning with their childhood and up to their present situation. Remind them that everyone has "stuff" and we all are in need of God's healing and unconditional love. Each person can share what he or she wants, but please be aware of the time. If there are too many people to do this within the time limits, you may have part of the group share during the first session and the other part during the second session.

NOTE: It is important, from the very first night, to hear people tell their story so you can see where they are coming from and what their issues may be. Many times, throughout the sessions, their hurt will go back to what they lived as a kid. That recognition will help them see the power those experiences have had on them and how they have affected their lives, feelings, decisions and relationships. Priceless!

Whenever someone gets emotional, have tissues available and allow them to process for a short time. Sometimes, a participant may get too emotional to share, so ask them if they want you to move on. Be sensitive because it may be embarrassing for them. If they need to, they can leave the room to collect themselves and then in a couple of minutes, a leader may go out and comfort them. Participants must feel free to "feel what they feel" and process through an issue.

Share the following stats as they fill in the blanks:

 # LINK OF TRUTH: DIVORCE STATS (page 3)

41 percent of first marriages will end in divorce.
60 percent of second marriages will end in divorce.
73 percent of subsequent marriages will end in divorce.
50 percent of American children will witness the divorce of their parents before age eighteen.
50 percent of children will also witness their parents' second divorce .
3 million unmarried couples are living together in the USA, an 80 percent increase since 1980. Note: There is a higher breakup rate for unmarried couples than for married couples.
40 percent of children in America live without a father in the home.
Source: *divorcerate.org*/Marriage Success Secrets

Explain that even though a participant's parents divorced, it does not mean that he or she is destined to experience his or her own divorce as an adult, even though statistics show that the vast majority do. One of the goals of this curriculum is to help break the pattern of divorce in families.

 # SMALL GROUPS

Go to pages 56-57 for small group instructions

Leaders, explain the purpose of small groups: Breaking into smaller groups divided by gender allows deeper conversations and connections. This also allows people to have more one-on-one time with leaders as they explore issues and feelings.

THIS WEEK:

Please allow adequate time for conversation (fifteen to twenty minutes).
Fill out and discuss "Links of Issues" (page 4) and "Links of Losses" (page 5)

 # PRAYER REQUESTS AND PRAISES – BIG GROUP

Please read Jeremiah 29:11–14a:

"'For I know the plans I have for you,' declares the Lord, 'plans to prosper you and not to harm you, plans to give you hope and a future. Then you will call upon Me and come and pray to Me, and I will listen to you. You will seek Me and find Me when you seek Me with all your heart. I will be found by you,' declares the Lord."

Appoint one of your leaders to keep a prayer journal for the group. Have them ask for prayer requests and praises, write them down, and then lead in prayer. You can have the same leader lead prayer time every week or take turns. These requests are confidential.

SUGGESTION:

At the end of the thirteen weeks, you can give each person a list of answered prayers to show them God's provision in His answers to requests and rejoice in the praises. This is a wonderful tool that encourages group members to trust that God is on the throne, loves them, and will provide for them.

NOTES

LINKS IN YOUR CHAIN
(Part Two)

IDENTIFYING

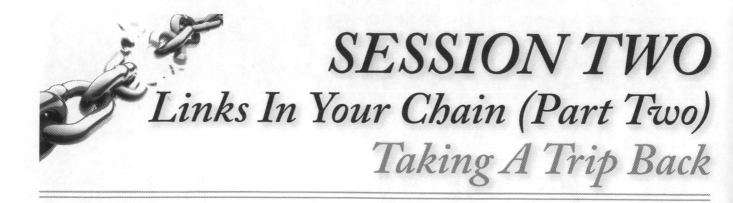

SESSION TWO
Links In Your Chain (Part Two)
Taking A Trip Back

Session Two is all about going back to the separation/divorce or death of their parents, remembering what it was like, revisiting how it felt, and identifying the pain that came from it. In this session, we will also look at the pattern of divorce in the families of group members.

SESSION GOALS

- Look back to the crisis and trauma of your parents' separation/divorce
- Explore your experience, how it affected those involved, and the emotions involved
- Look at the possible family patterns of marriage and divorce in your immediate and extended family and how they affect you

GROUP GAB

1. Welcome group members.
2. Review safety and respect guidelines.
3. Go over their session title page (page 8), including the verse.
4. Ask the following questions (quick answers)
    a. How old were you when your parents divorced?
    b. Do or did you think a divorce might happen to you someday, too?
    c. Have you gotten a divorce?
    d. What do you think it takes to have a lifelong healthy marriage?
    e. Do you think a healthy marriage is possible for you? Why or why not?

SMALL GROUPS

Please explain that these pages are necessary to bring participants back to the actual experience of their parents' separation/divorce so they can begin to see the power it has had over them in their decisions, beliefs, attitudes, and emotional issues up to this point in their lives. Please take your time on these pages.

1. Have participants fill out "The Chains of Your Parents' Divorce" (page 9-10) and "Family Footprints" (page 11). Go over their answers. This is a great way for group members to connect with one another and realize that their experiences are not isolated ones. You may wish to play some soothing instrumental music.
2. You might find that these pages will affect participants now because their own children have experienced or are experiencing your participants' divorce.
3. Please be prepared for some emotional responses as your group opens the box of immense pain they may have put away for a long time.

LINK OF TRUTH: LINKS TO YOUR PARENTS' DIVORCE – BIG GROUP

One of the most important truths of this study is that no matter what you have experienced, you do not have to define yourself by it. Whether you have been through abuse of any kind, isolation or abandonment, abortion, incarceration, bad choices, the horrid damage from your parents' separation/divorce, or even your own divorce, God made you, knows you, sees you, and loves and accepts you.

You may not feel that right now. You may not feel worthy of such unconditional love, but hopefully, through this study, you will be able to base your self-worth on God's amazing love for you and not what anyone or anything has ever told you.

You may know these truths in your mind, but it hasn't been transferred to your heart, so you may not feel God's love or care for you. You may feel like God is far away or has turned His back on you. You may feel that, but it is not the truth.

The Lord has provided caring *Chained No More* leaders who will walk you through this journey, led by the Holy Spirit. They will not beat you over the head with the Bible but will consistently lead you to His Word for truth that will overshadow the lies, betrayal, and hurt from your past. "You will know the truth and the truth shall set you free" (John 8:32).

Truth is first of all a quality that belongs to God—to Christ and the Spirit. God wants truth developed in us. We must *seek* it, *speak* it, *walk* in it, *live* by it, and *worship* in it, because only then will we be truly free.

PRAYER REQUESTS AND PRAISES

NOTES

UNDERSTANDING THE LINKS

CONNECTIONS

SESSION THREE
Understanding The Links
The Chain Of Grief

Session Three will be about looking at the chain of grief and exploring where each member is right now on that chain. It will also look more closely at the links of denial and bargaining. There is also a portion of this session on the subject of betrayal and trust, since these are subjects children of divorce wrestle with whether they are eight or eighty years old.

LEADER NOTE:

Please realize that those in your class are still learning to trust you, and just because you say something, that doesn't make it truth. Make sure you know the material in each session and are well-prepared. Feel free to use other Scripture when studying for class. Your class deserves your best—and certainly the Lord Jesus does!

 SESSION GOALS

- Begin to look at the "Chain of Grief"
- Recognize where you think you are at this point on that chain
- Explore the denial and bargaining portions of the "Chain of Grief" and see how you may have used these in the past and may be still using them today
- Look at the subjects of betrayal and trust and how they may still be playing out in your life today

 GROUP GAB

1. Welcome group members.
2. Ask participants what the best part of their day was.
3. Introduce the subjects of denial and bargaining. Go over their session title page (page 14), including the verse.
4. Read the top of page 15 aloud and have students put an *X* that represents their location on the "Chain of Grief" and share that with the group. Explain that this chain is slippery, meaning that they can slide back and forth on the chain, depending on memories coming up, or family dynamics, holidays, family weddings, funerals, etc.

 LINK OF TRUTH: DENIAL AND BARGAINING

DEFINITION OF DENIAL: a negotiation in logic or a refusal to admit the truth or reality. Denial is a protective emotion that shields you from pain. Denial can mean anything from avoiding the subject of the divorce, to focusing on others, to always keeping busy and never slowing down enough to feel or talk.

DEFINITION OF BARGAINING: testing whether something is open to negotiation or may be reversible. Bargaining could have included trying to get your parents to seek help for their marriage, attempting to be a peacemaker or mediator between your parents, or causing problems so your parents would focus on you and not their relationship issues.

None of these ways of bargaining can work, because the issue of divorce was between your parents, and nothing you could say or do would ultimately keep them together. It was neither your fault nor your problem to fix.

 # SMALL GROUPS

Have the group fill out the "Denial and Bargaining" and "Betrayal/Trust" (pages 16, 17) and then have them discuss what they have discovered.

This is a good time to talk about how we pray to God (i.e. use Him as a candy store, a complaint department, a whipping post, a close friend, the Almighty God, etc.) Remind them they can transfer these questions to their own divorce, if they wish.

Also talk with participants about how we need to listen to God through His Word and His Holy Spirit as well. Usually, we do most or all of the talking and very little (if any) listening. A close relationship requires both talking and listening.

 # LINK OF TRUTH: BETRAYAL AND TRUST
- BIG GROUP

Trust is something that is earned and not a right. From the moment you were born, you had to trust your parent(s) to clothe and feed you—to meet your every need. One day, trust was broken when your parents separated and divorced.

Maybe you lost your trust in people in general, in God, or in the thought of love and marriage. Your dream for a healthy family was shattered, and maybe you didn't know who to trust. Maybe your mom said one thing and your dad said another. Who do you believe?

Eventually, you couldn't deny the divorce or try to manipulate your way out of it. It was reality!

Go over "God's Idea of Trust (page 18) as a group.

 # PRAYER REQUESTS AND PRAISES

NOTE: Don't forget to look back and see how the Lord has been faithful to answer prayer from previous weeks and what can still be prayed for. Seeing how He works things for our good builds our faith and trust in Him.

NOTES

POWER OF THE CHAIN

"His divine power has given us everything we need for life and godliness through our knowledge of Him who called us by His own glory and goodness, through these He has given us His very great and precious promises, so that through them, you may participate in the divine nature and escape the corruption in the world caused by evil desires"   (2 Peter 1:3–4).

SESSION FOUR
Power Of The Chain
Family Patterns And Their Effects

Session Four is a deep and involved session that will help your class explore the parenting they had and its effects on them. It is important to look back and see where our current attitudes and issues may have come from so we can see the power they have had on us.

LEADER NOTE:

This session could bring up strong emotions as well as stories of abuse. Please use wisdom and discretion in the class. If you feel it is necessary, you can take someone aside for more one-on-one time to help them process but not offend others.

 SESSION GOALS

- To explore your family's patterns of divorce
- To look at the issues in your family and how your family dealt or deals with them and then see how you have continued or broken those patterns in your personal life
- To look at the positive/negative effect your parents have had on you
- To explore the issues of keeping secrets concerning your parents' divorce and the effect those secrets have on you today
- To look at what was/is your fault and what was/is in your control and out of your control

 GROUP GAB

1. Welcome group members.
2. Ask participants what their idea of a perfect parent is.
3. If anyone is a parent, ask him or her if he or she sees any similarities (good or bad) between the way he or she parents and how he or she was parented.
4. Go over their session title page (page 20), including the verse.

 LINK OF TRUTH: FAMILY PATTERNS

We are all a product of our parenting—good or bad. Some of us had caring parents, whether they divorced or not. Some of us had abusive parents or neglectful parents. There is nothing we can do to change our past now, but it is important to explore the parenting we had and how it has affected us up to this point in our lives. When we do that, we can make the choice to continue those patterns or break the chains for generations ahead.

What is your idea of a perfect parent? Would your description include a parent who spent time with you, talked with you and not at you, was kind and caring? They taught and trained you for your adult life, respected you, were honest with you, valued your family and laughed with you. Many of us have had that kind of parent, but many of us have not.

Once again, you may have had a parent or parents who were not available to you, abused you, neglected you, and never made you feel you had much value. It is common for children to define themselves by what their parents told them or did to them negatively and just resign to the fact that they will do the same thing. You do not have to define yourself by what happened to you as a child, whether it is divorce, abuse, putdowns or anything else.

As you explore the patterns in your family, be encouraged, not discouraged because you are on a path of healing and freedom. This is the next step toward a much more positive future where you can make a difference in a positive way. Even if someone told you that you would amount to nothing or that you were a loser or any number of other horrible putdowns, IT IS NOT TRUE! "All things are possible to them who love God."

Please fill out "Family Page" (page 21) and the "Livin' In the House" (page 22). Let each person share one of his or her patterns. It is important for them to recognize if they have carried a pattern forward or broken it in their lives.

Now have them fill out the "What About Parenting" (page 23) and discuss.

LEADER NOTE: Please allow at least half an hour for these pages to be filled out and discussed.

SMALL GROUPS

Introduction: Many kids of divorce are expected to keep secrets between their parents and also lie about what the "other parent" is doing. Kids are put right in the middle and taught at an early age how to be untruthful, spy on others, and develop an overall sense of mistrust.

Loyalty issues are huge with kids of divorce. They may have wondered, "Who should I go to live with? What if I tell Dad that Mom has a boyfriend? What if I really like Dad's new friend? Will that hurt Mom's feelings?" and on and on ...

Have your group fill out "Secrets and Lies" (pages 24-25), and let them discuss it. Remind them that they can fill this page out looking at their own divorce and what their kids experienced.

NOTE: Some participants may still be expected to play this game between their parents, so talk to them about getting themselves off their parents' battlefield and not being a part of it anymore. Suggest that they use a firm but kind voice and say, *"Mom/Dad, I have been going between both of you for a long time, and it is time that I step off of your battlefield and let you deal with your own issues together. I will not be keeping secrets for either of you, lying for you, or spying on the other for you anymore. I want to be free to love you both."*

What your parents choose to do with their relationship from then on is up to the two of them. Maybe they would realize they need to resolve their own issues and not rely on you to be their mediator. Maybe they would just decide it isn't worth it anymore and completely separate. In stepping off their battlefield and not being manipulated anymore, you have no more responsibility for that and you can move forward and break that link in your chain.

LINK OF TRUTH: IT'S NOT YOUR FAULT-BIG GROUP

Many kids think that for some reason, their parents' divorce was partially or entirely their fault. Some kids only hear one side of the story or aren't told the reason for the divorce until much later in life. Usually they will hear a biased account of what happened, and the children stand between the parents in confusion.

Truth: Nothing you could have done would have prevented your parents' divorce. It was their choice and their choice alone!

Fill out the "It's Not My Fault!" (page 26).

Have everyone in the class say, with passion, "It's not my fault!" three times.

PRAYER REQUESTS AND PRAISES

NOTES

GRIP OF THE CHAIN

ANGER

SESSION FIVE
Grip Of The Chain
Recognizing Anger

Session Five is all about recognizing anger, its effects, and how we deal with it. You will be able to give some tools to help your group deal with it more effectively.

LEADER NOTE:

Be aware of strong emotions. Some of your participants may still be dealing with the anger toward their parents or in other relationships at the present time. Many times, people will carry the pattern of anger into their adult relationships, because that is what they are familiar with and feel they deserve. Be open to suggesting resources in your church or community (ie. Christian counselors, therapists, social services, pastors, etc.) to help them get away from abusive relationships or work on anger issues at a deeper level than you can provide. It is vitally important that participants work through their anger before it affects other people and other relationships.

 ## SESSION GOALS

- Focus on getting a grip on your anger before it grips *you*
- Identify our reactions to anger as well as what sets us off
- Discuss our anger at God and how we can deal with that
- Find healthy ways to diffuse our anger

 ## GROUP GAB

1. Welcome group members.
2. Have each person share three things the class doesn't know about him or her. Go over their session title page (page 28), including the verse..
3. Have each person share one of the times he or she got very angry and what he or she did (can be any age and funny or not).

 ## LINK OF TRUTH: ANGER

Anger is a natural response to hurt, fear, or not getting your own way. Beneath the anger, though, is mostly hurt. Anger is an emotion that can be easy to get into but very hard to get out of. It can build and build or it can catch us off guard. You may have been raised around a lot of anger and you saw and felt the results of that. You may also find that you are "just like your dad/mom" when it comes to anger and you may want to change that pattern but don't know how. Many times, people will carry the pattern of anger from their childhood into their adult relationships because that is what they are familiar with and feel they deserve.

You may still be mad at one or both of your parents or others and you may have some very good reasons to be angry. *Being angry isn't necessarily wrong, but what you do with it can be very wrong.*

For some of us, the grip of anger has held us for so long that it is almost like a "comfortable shoe" and we see no other way to look at things. It has clouded our thinking to the point that we almost define ourselves by it. Maybe you are surrounded by angry people or those who express rage on a daily basis. There is a cloud of anger over your everyday environment. Somehow you got in that environment and you have seen yourself change into an angry person as well.

You may also be mad at God for letting things happen in your family or other areas of your life. You may even blame Him. The truth is again, that God gives us a free will and didn't "make" anyone hurt you. He didn't cause the breakup of your family; people in your family did. He didn't cause your abuse; human beings did and many times, their anger or actions came from their own deep hurt.

For some of us, we are really good at hiding the anger we feel. We put a happy face on and no one would ever know that inside, just under the surface, or even way down deep, there is a rage burning in us. Sound familiar?

"What causes fights and quarrels among you? Don't they come from your desires that battle within you? You want something, but don't get it." (James 4:1–2a)

Anger can be a good emotion, because it can protect us and lets us know when we've been hurt or wronged. It also allows us to stand up for ourselves. The problem comes when we keep it all in until it gets to a point where we can't control our anger or we are so scared of becoming angry that we under-react by stuffing our anger and try to convince ourselves that we're not angry. Stuffing your anger can be just as harmful as overreacting.
—Krista Smith, *The Big D: Divorce Thru the Eyes of a Teen*

Go over "Anger Thermometer" (page 29) with the entire group. They can use the words *irritating, boiling, rage,* etc.

 # SMALL GROUPS

Have your group fill out and go over the "What Ticks You Off?" (page 30) and then go over "Link of Truth" (page 31) and discuss.

LEADER NOTE: On "What Ticks You Off" (page 30), help participants go deeper to see why some things anger them more than others (e.g. favoritism, because a younger sibling was the "good," "intelligent," or "pretty" child).

Have them fill out "Signs of Anger" and "Managing Your Anger" (page 32-34)

Go over "God's Word on Anger" (page 35) as a big group for your closing discussion time.

 # PRAYER REQUESTS AND PRAISES

Ask the participants if there is an issue regarding anger they would like you to pray about so they can have healing and resolution.

NOTES

UNDER THE GRIP OF THE CHAIN

WHAT'S REALLY GOING ON?

SESSION SIX
Under The Grip Of The Chain
Exploring What Is Behind Anger

Session Six is a session that will help you begin to dig deep into what the true emotions are concerning the divorce of participants' parents and other issues. We will look below the surface of anger to where the hurt really lies. It is important that you continue to remind the group that the battle between their parents or any abuse was not their fault and because they may have been a child at the time, they were the most victimized. That *is* something to be sad about!

LEADER NOTE:

There may be some who cannot face their feelings and want to walk out or just isolate themselves during some of this session. Encourage them to face their feelings however they need to, but after a little while, come alongside them and encourage them. You might even ask them if you can pray with them about what they feel. Be sensitive, and don't rush this part of the process; let the Holy Spirit guide you. Make sure you have tissues available for this session.

 ## SESSION GOALS

- Learn what is *really* under anger
- Become familiar with the names of many emotions
- Identify the worries you felt as a result of your parents' divorce
- Identify the emotions you are feeling and release your pain

 ## GROUP GAB

1. Welcome group members
2. Introduce the theme by going over their session title page (page 38), including the verse.
3. Give each student an 8½ x 11-inch piece of paper, and have him or her write the alphabet down the left side of the page. Now have each participant write an emotion using each of the letters. Go to http://e-id.vagabondgirl.net/index.php?letter-K for a big list of emotions.

LINK OF TRUTH: EMOTIONS

There are literally hundreds of emotions we feel throughout our lives. Many times, we generally label them as only a few: angry, happy, sad, confused, frustrated, etc.

When we look deeper, we can identify these emotions for what they are and then truly deal with them. We may be angry because someone cancelled on us, and this could mean we are really disappointed or are feeling lonely. In this example, anger could cause us to ignore the person who cancelled plans, write the person off, or blow up at him or her, whereas disappointment or loneliness might cause us to try to resolve the situation.

Another way we "deal" with emotions is to just put them aside, ignore them and try to move on. We may say that the person who hurt us is not worth it or we don't want to cause more problems. We may think we just have to "forgive and forget", but what happens is that it prevents us from dealing with it, resolving the conflict, only to have resentment resurface later. Over years of not resolving the issue, it can cause us to have a root of bitterness and we can never be free of it.

Another way we can many times "deal with" difficult situations is to worry. Oh, we worry about the economy, whether our kids will do well in life, whether our spouse really loves us as much as they say they do, our health, politics, where we are going to get our next meal, if we are safe, if we are ever going to get out of this situation/relationship, etc. etc. etc. We can even worry about being worried for heaven's sake! Worry causes stress, stress causes health problems and a myriad of other issues.

Do you realize that every single moment that we worry, we are saying to God, "I don't trust You with my little life. You can't handle all I go through. Your promises are not true for me"?

SMALL GROUPS

Have the students fill out "Anger Umbrella" (pages 39-40) and discuss it. Now have them explore the subject of "Worry" (page 41), and make sure to ask them to dig a little deeper and explain why these things worried them so much. Ask them to reflect on and discuss how these worries might still be issues for them now. Some may transfer these issues to what they put their children through in their own divorce and this can be very painful for them. Remind them that they can't change that now, but maybe later, after finishing this class, they may be able to go to their kids and truly admit to the pain they caused their kids and ask for their forgiveness.

LINK OF TRUTH: LINKS OF PAIN – BIG GROUP

ACTIVITY INTRODUCTION: We have all suffered many hurts throughout our lives, and some of those were a direct result of our parents. Some of the hurts we have are a result of our own actions, and some are completely out of our control. These hurts have been chains around our minds and hearts. This exercise will give you a picture of the amount of hurt there is in our class but will also show that Jesus is in the midst of it. He cares about you and loves you.

LEADER NOTE:
- Make at least thirty light gray strips of paper per participant (8½ x 2 inches).
- Have a black permanent marker or glue stick available for each person.
- Make at least seven red strips per person with the name of Jesus written in bold letters and a heart drawn on either end.
- Have the participants write one hurt on each gray strip. Glue the strips into links.
- Between every five gray links, insert a red Jesus link. This is to remind them that Jesus was there through all of the experiences.
- Let the participants know this chain will be brought back in a later session.
- Connect all the chains together with a black link to help them see the chains the enemy has covered them with as individuals as well as the entire group. Powerful visual!
- If you feel comfortable, have everyone lay hands on the entire chain and pray that God will break the chains and bring healing and freedom as they move forward through sessions.

PRAYER REQUESTS AND PRAISES

NOTES

WEIGHT OF THE CHAIN

DEPRESSION

SESSION SEVEN
Weight Of The Chain
Facing Depression

Session Seven is a lesson that will help participants face the depression they have felt throughout their lives. Depression may be the reason some of them have decided to come to *Chained No More*. They may be looking for answers on how to move ahead without it.

It is also important to see if the participants' deep sadness or lingering depression began with the divorce of their parents. Help them explore this possibility.

LEADER NOTE:

Be sensitive to the possibility of suicidal thoughts. Listen to the participants and see if there are some verbal clues that they are near the edge. If you are concerned about someone's suicidal tendencies, talk with that person, and if necessary, contact a professional, a pastor, or your local suicide hotline immediately. Also, suggest that a participant call the suicide hotline or seek out personal counseling.

Try to give participants hope, but refrain from giving them pat "Christian" answers, such as, "All things work together for good for them who love God" (Romans 8:28). This verse is true; however, it may seem uncaring and trite at this time.

 SESSION GOALS

- Discuss depression, what it is, and what it looks like
- Look at the different levels of depression and recognize where you are
- Discuss healthy and unhealthy ways to cope with depression

 GROUP GAB

1. Welcome group members.
2. Introduce the theme by going over their session title page (44), including the verse.
3. Have participants fill out "Weight of the Chain" (45) as well as "Reasons for Your Depression" (46). Participants may add more levels to their chain of depression if they wish. If someone is not depressed at this time, he or she may be able to think of a time when he or she was and use that for answers to explore it.

 LINK OF TRUTH: DEPRESSION

We have all felt depression at one time or another in our lives. Sometimes it may be a day when we feel down and don't really want to leave the house. Sometimes, it can drop us into a deep valley and we CAN'T leave the house for a long period of time. It can affect our jobs, relationships, health and virtually every area of our life. You may look around and see happy families, celebrations, and others seeming to enjoy life so much more than you do. Life seems to be passing you by while you are stuck in this fog.

Depression is a big part of the chain of grief. It may last for just a short time or sometimes, it can last for years. Depression is more than merely being sad. It is a lack of hope. Depression can be anything from a lingering sadness to suicidal thoughts.

Maybe you sleep too much or don't sleep at all. Some people have an increased appetite, and some can hardly eat at all. No matter what level of depression you might feel, if it is left unattended for a long time, it can be very harmful to your entire well-being.

Depression can last for a few months and begin with feeling a little blue. It can eventually make you feel like giving up. It is part of the chain of grief. You may come out of it for a while, and then something may bring you right back down.

It is part of the process toward healing. This class may have even brought you back to depression by reminding you of a very sad time in your life—but know that you are headed toward healing.

Depression can last a relatively long time and eventually slip you into clinical depression. If it is severe or longstanding, it may be appropriate to have a doctor prescribe medicine to help you cope or seek out other resources (counseling, spiritual disciplines, social relationships) as well.

STEP 1—Recognize and acknowledge you may be depressed.
STEP 2—Have a desire to find some answers and get better.
STEP 3—Get out there, and don't isolate yourself. Get involved with a hobby, a sport, or serve in your local church or community in a tangible way. Be careful, though, not to get so busy that you cover the depression and do not deal with it.
STEP 4—See a doctor, and follow his or her instructions.
STEP 5—See a pastor who uses God's Word, counselor, or therapist to talk things out at length.

 # SMALL GROUPS

Have your group fill out "Depression and You" and "Depression: What Do You Do?" (pages 47-48). Discuss both. Make the discussion of the second page more lighthearted, if possible.

As a big group, ask the students to give their ideas on what works for them when they get depressed. Go over "God Understands Depression" with the participants (page 49).

LEADER NOTE: Plan a social outing during the coming week to connect students on a social level (e.g. pizza, a movie, a ball game, a BBQ, etc.). There are a lot of heavy subjects in this program, and it is a good idea to balance that out with some fun as a group too. Keep conversation light during the activity, and have fun!

 # PRAYER REQUESTS AND PRAISES

NOTES

GOD'S LINK TO YOU

"The Lord is the shelter for the oppressed, a refuge in time of trouble. Those who know Your name trust in You, for You, O Lord, have never abandoned anyone who searches for You."
(Psalm 9:9–10)

SESSION EIGHT
God's Link To You
Who God Is To You

Session Eight begins the journey of healing and renewal as we look at God's Word. We will find out who God is, what He thinks of us, and how to receive His salvation and acceptance into His family.

LEADER NOTE:

Please be ready to give your testimony about when you accepted Christ and how He has changed your life. If you have never given your testimony before, practice it at home before this session.

SESSION GOALS

· Define who we are aside from the past
· Discuss who God is to us and where that belief came from
· Compare our earthly parents to God, the heavenly Father, through the truth of the Word
· Write a letter to God

GROUP GAB

1. Welcome group members.
2. Introduce the theme by going over their session title page (page 52), including the verse.
3. Give each student and leader a 3 x 5-inch card, and have each write his or her first name down the left-hand side of the card. Provide them with pencils so they can erase if they need to. Now have them write something about themselves using the letters of their names. This is something they are and *not* what they do. For example, *Kim* might be *kind, imaginative,* and *messy.* Give them a few minutes to do this, and then have them share with the group. This is fun!

NOTE: This may be difficult for some individuals, because they may not be used to thinking of themselves in a positive way. You may give them ideas by telling them good things you see in them. Remind them that all that is good in us is there because it was placed by God, and we need to keep that in mind.

LINK OF TRUTH: OUR FAITH

NOTE: If a participant comes up with some belief that is different from the truth of the Bible, don't react. Remember that it is the Holy Spirit's job to change a heart; not ours. They must feel safe to share how they feel and what they believe. We don't, however, want to turn the class into a religious debate, so guard against that.

What do you believe in? Do you believe in God, or do you have a different belief system? Do you believe the Bible is the Word of God? What has God done for you?

These are questions we all wrestle with at some time in our lives. We may wrestle with them throughout our lives, depending what is going on. Maybe you gave your heart to Jesus when you were a child in Sunday school, or maybe you made a commitment when you were a teen at summer camp or a big youth event. You may have accepted Christ as an adult, or maybe you haven't put your faith in Him yet. Whatever the case, God created you, sees you, knows you, has

0

Chained No More

never taken His eye off of you, and wants to have a loving relationship with you. God has a purpose for you, and this purpose remains the same no matter how your circumstances change throughout your life.

God didn't cause the problems you have had in your life, but He was always nearby to help you through them. He could have prevented those challenges, but for some reason, He did not. We will talk about some possible good things that have come from your past in a later session.

It is our nature to let our circumstances or the opinions/expectations of others determine our self-worth, instead of basing it on who God says we are. Think about it...*we allow people who are as flawed and fickle as we are to determine our value.* How sad it that?

Whether we were made fun of as a little kid, put down as a teen or hurt deeply in relationships, we have all been hurt at one time or another. Teens will try to "fill the void" and they will gravitate to the people and places that make them feel accepted and valued, which could mean connecting with other hurting kids with negative behavior. This can cause children to isolate themselves, self-medicate or can even work extra hard to be successful. Inside, they are crumbling and do not feel they are worthy of someone's love, time or even worthy to live.

The church is filled with imperfect people just like you and me, who have daily struggles, no matter how nice they look walking into the church building on Sundays. If you are going to look at human beings, in or out of the church, you will always be able to see flaws and inconsistencies.

God didn't cause the problems you have had in your life, but He was always nearby to help you through them if you were to ask Him. *This* Father will not walk away, hurt you, yell at you, abuse you, ignore you or treat you like you are nothing. *This* Father does not keep records of all of our mistakes and bad decisions. *This* Father loves you for exactly who you are. You don't need to be perfect to come to Him and build a relationship with Him. Praying is just talking to *this* Father, sharing your feelings and thoughts, seeking Him for answers and praising Him for who He is. Let Him have your heart.

"I know the plans I have for you,' declares the Lord, 'plans to prosper you and not to harm you. Plans to give you hope and a future. Then you will call upon Me and come and pray to Me and I will listen to you. You will seek Me and find Me when you seek Me with all your heart." (Jeremiah 29:11–13)

SMALL GROUPS

Please have your group fill out the "God and You" section on (page 53).

LEADER NOTE: "Who's Your Daddy?" (page 54) is a very important page to go over. Many people find it difficult to trust in a heavenly Father they *can't* see when they couldn't trust in the earthly fathers or mothers they *could* see. *Please stop and pray with your group before you go over this page.* Pray that the Holy Spirit will open their eyes and hearts to the truth of the Word about our heavenly Father. Have a leader read the left column and have participants take turns reading the right column so they speak truth out of their mouth. Powerful!

SOLO TIME

Let each person find a place to be alone to write a letter to God. Provide them with paper. Even if some haven't put their faith in God, they may have questions or things to say to Him. This is entirely private and should not be shared. It is important that we communicate with God and come to Him with what is on our hearts. Put on some soft instrumental music during this activity. He hears you, sees you, knows you, cares about you, and loves you.

When they have finished their letter to God, come back as a group and go over "God's Care for You", page (55). Have a leader read the scripture in Psalm 139 out loud with expression as they listen.

PRAYER REQUESTS AND PRAISES

NOTES

LETTING GO OF THE CHAIN

FORGIVENESS

SESSION NINE
Letting Go Of The Chain
Receiving And Giving Forgiveness

Session Nine may be a very healing session, as we explore God's forgiveness for us and take powerful steps to forgive the pain people and circumstances have caused us. It is important for us to understand what forgiveness is and what it is not. We need to understand how much we can be held down by the chains of unforgiveness and be willing to begin this vital part of our healing process.

<u>LEADER NOTE:</u>

Some participants may feel like they have forgiven their parents or other people, but whenever they think about them or the circumstances, their thoughts bring up strong negative feelings. Emotions can sometimes follow the act of forgiveness years later. Please go to the Robyn B ministries website (www.robynbministries.com). Download "Forgiveness Quotes" and give them out prior to doing the "cross activity".

 ## SESSION GOALS

- Explore and define what forgiveness is and what it isn't
- Discuss the depth of God's forgiveness for us
- Look at areas of our lives where unforgiveness has chained us down
- Break the chain of unforgiveness in our lives
- Experience God's grace and be able to give grace to others

 ## GROUP GAB

1. Welcome group members.
2. Introduce the theme by going over their session title page (page 58), including the verse.
3. Have each person fill out "How Do You Spell Forgiveness" (page 59), and then have them share their answers.

🔗 LINK OF TRUTH: FORGIVENESS

Forgiveness is a big subject, and there are many opinions about what we will forgive and what we won't.

Why is it so hard to forgive some people and easier to forgive others? Maybe because the level of forgiveness depends on the level of pain someone caused us. Hurts like betrayal, abandonment, or abuse of any kind can be harder to forgive than a lie, miscommunication, embarrassment, etc.

Sometimes, the hurt is too great and we continue to live in the darkness of bitterness and unforgiveness. Living with unforgiveness can be a cancer on our heart and affect layers upon layers in our life. Bitterness is kind of like another cover emotion which hides issues such as hurt, fear, embarrassment, betrayal, abandonment and so forth. If we "hang our hat" on bitterness and unforgiveness, then we may never really look at and deal with the issues under it, which keeps us from being free. More chains.

No matter what the offense was, it is important to take steps toward forgiveness. Forgiving others doesn't take *them* off the hook as much as it takes *you* off the hook.

That doesn't mean you necessarily forget the offense either. Some things are just too painful to forget, right? It means you say, **"I release you from the pain you caused me; it will have no power over me anymore!"**

You see, when you remain in unforgiveness and anger, you are still giving the person who offended you power over you on some pretty deep levels. You are allowing them to take your joy, freedom, and peace of mind. You are allowing them to make you feel less than your best. You are allowing them to make you keep score as well as the desire to "settle the score", which God says is His to settle.

Let's explore the subject of forgiveness now.

Have the class do "Forgiveness—Right or Wrong" and "Forgiveness—Fact or Fiction?" (pages 60-61) and discuss.

LEADER NOTE: This may be where you can give your testimony about putting your faith in Jesus Christ and how He has changed your life.

 # SMALL GROUPS

INTRO: Let's take a turn now and look at Jesus and all those who hated Him, spit on Him, ridiculed Him, and hurt Him in almost every way possible. Why did He allow that to happen when He could have taken a breath and obliterated all of them in an instant? Why did He allow Himself to be dragged through the streets in front of thousands and then be placed on a huge wooden cross with His hands and feet nailed to that cross with spikes and then raised up so all could see and then said, "Father, forgive them"?

Why did He do that? Because that is what His Heavenly Father asked of Him and because He was enduring all of this to make payment for the sins of all of us through time. Humanly speaking, it is beyond comprehension why someone would do that for me or anyone else. This is not some gory story; it is TRUTH and it is for you right here and right now.

Have your group fill out "God's Forgiveness to You" (page 62) and go over "The Sinner's Prayer" and "Growing in God" (page 64).

BIG GROUP: Please go over "God's Truth on Forgiveness" (page 63) with them and invite them to accept the Lord or come back to Him.

LEADERS: Bring out the gray "Links of Pain" from session six. Have participants find the links they personally wrote, and then remove them from the chain. Have a large poster board cross cut out or smaller crosses for each person, as well as some double-sided tape or glue sticks. You may also make a wooden cross with long spikes on it; whatever works for your class. Participants should have privacy when doing this activity, to allow for deep emotions with no distractions. Please allow as much time as possible for this activity.

ACTIVITY INTRO: We made this chain to signify the hurts we have carried in our lives. These are the hurts that have affected us and held us back from joy and freedom in our lives. It is time to lay those hurts at the foot of the cross and be willing to forgive those who have hurt us.

We have been given the gift of forgiveness from Jesus, and now we can give the gift of forgiveness to others as well as to ourselves. Find all of your links, and remove them from the chain. If you can take that link, recognize the person who caused you the pain and say, **"I release you from the pain you caused me. It WILL have no power over me... anymore!"** Now take a piece of tape or a glue stick and put that link on the cross. There may be some they cannot forgive yet, so keep those links until they can put them on the cross too. Pray with them about that.

When the participants have finished putting their links on the cross, LEADERS, lay your hands on the cross and pray about them being able to release these chains once and for all. Pray that the Lord will give them freedom in Him now.

Explain to participants that there may be times when they begin thinking about these hurts again. *We can't help our first thoughts, but sure can help our second thoughts and dwelling on something.* That is the time to say out loud, "No, I put that on the cross and I am NOT taking it back! Lord, I laid it at Your feet and it will stay there! The enemy will have no power over me and these will not have any power over me anymore, in the name of Jesus. I stand in the strength of Jesus Christ."

When they are done with their "Links of Pain", please ask them to look at page 65 and explore other areas of forgiveness in their lives.

 # PRAYER REQUESTS AND PRAISES

LEADER NOTE: If anyone has accepted Christ as Savior during this session, have him or her share that with the class, if he or she is willing. Be sure to rejoice with this person and welcome him or her into the family of God. Remind the person that the Bible says the angels rejoice in heaven when one comes to Him. In other words, there's a party in heaven for him or her! Praise the Lord!

NOTES

NOTES

BREAKING THE CHAIN

*"If you hold to My teaching, you are really My disciples.
Then you will know the truth and the truth will set you free!"*
(John 8:31–32)

SESSION TEN
Breaking The Chain
Discovering The REAL You

Session Ten will probably be a very fun, freeing, and insightful session, because it deals with who we truly are aside from our past. It will begin with a fun exercise in which participants share things about themselves and also look at some positive things that may have come out of their parents' divorce or other painful experiences.

The next step is to explore what the participants' spiritual gifts are and who God says they are in His Word. Enjoy.

 ## SESSION GOALS

· Recognize the positive things about yourself
· Define who God wants you to be
· Look at some of the positive things that may have come from the divorce of your parents
· Discover your spiritual gifts
· Discover what God's Word says about His children

 ## GROUP GAB

1. Welcome group members.
2. Go over their session title page (page 68), including the verse.
3. Have each person give three words that would describe himself or herself. Then add one word *you* think describes each of them.
4. Now have participants fill out "Freedom to Be Me" (page 69) and share their answers. Make this fun.

 ## LINK OF TRUTH: NOT BAD AT ALL

You may have heard the saying, "God loves you and has a wonderful plan for your life"—a life not defined by the divorce of your parents or what you have endured.

Some of you can barely remember when times were good, and some of you have many good memories to hang onto. Those memories will always be a part of you; however, they don't have to define you.

Let's get right down to the basics...do you like who you are, what you look like, the state of your life right now? If you look in the mirror, are you pleased with what you see? That crooked smile, droopy eyelid, your buck teeth, or any number of other flaws are just that...flaws. We all have them. They don't define the person you are, even though other kids may have made fun of you when you were growing up. Remember the old saying "Sticks and stones may break my bones, but words will never hurt me"? Well, most of the time, words can hurt more than physical harm and the damage from those words can last a lifetime. We take it in and it can be used to stop us from being our best. More chains.

It begins to affect our self-value even as an adult. Why? Because deep within each of us, we want to be loved and accepted. We want people to like us and value us just for who we are. We don't want to have to put on faces and change them to impress people or groups we come in contact with. We want to be real, don't we? Or, maybe we are afraid of the real us.

Many times, because of our damage, we put up huge, thick walls around us so we won't be hurt again. The problem is, even though we think we are protecting ourselves, we are actually preventing any outsiders from really knowing us; the real us.

They may see a smile, but not know we are breaking inside. They may also see a hard exterior and not make the effort to really get to know us. We are actually "shooting ourselves in the foot" and then we lament because we don't have many friends. Some of us just finally give up and say, "I don't need friends; I am fine with my life."

Even though the pain of your parents' divorce or other painful experiences may have been overwhelming at times, you may now be able to see some positives that came from them too (e.g. more peace in the house with no more conflict, closer relationships with your brothers or sisters, becoming more responsible, stronger or more independent, etc.). Instead of dwelling only on the hurt or the conflict, let's look at what good may have come out of the divorce or other hurts in your life.

In this session, we want to explore who you really are. You are unique! You have gifts, talents, a specific temperament and spiritual gifts that you could use to help others and glorify God with.

Think of this session as a wrapped gift you are going to be opening. Inside this magnificent present, you will find the beautiful truths of who you are without all the garbage that came before. This is the truth about you. Leave all the negative messages you have heard and lived with for so many years and keep them outside of this present. There is no place for them here. You are who God says you are; nothing more and nothing less.

 # SMALL GROUPS

Have people fill out "Not So Bad ..." and "Pluses and Minuses" (pages 70,71) and discuss.

LEADER NOTE: Let students know that there are other gifts that are mentioned in the Bible, but these are the ones that we are focusing on and not the lesser gifts that may cause controversy in the class because of differing beliefs.

Have participants fill out "Spiritual Gifts" (page 72) to help them identify a very important part of their identity. Encourage them to find a place to use their spiritual gifts for the glory of God and maybe give them suggestions (ie. Their local church, mission, youth ministry, childcare). Please be careful how you present spiritual gifts because there are varying beliefs on it. Don't get on a soapbox; it's not yours to get on. Let them discover what He has for them.

BIG GROUP: "Identity Theft" (page 73) is important to go over, because it puts our identity, significance, and self-concept where it should be—in who God says we are. You can read the left column and have participants read the right column out loud together so they speak truth.

 # PRAYER REQUESTS AND PRAISES

NOTES

LOVE LINKS
LOVE & RELATIONSHIPS

"LOVE...bears all things, believes all things, hopes all things, endures all things. Love NEVER fails."
1 Corinthians 1:13

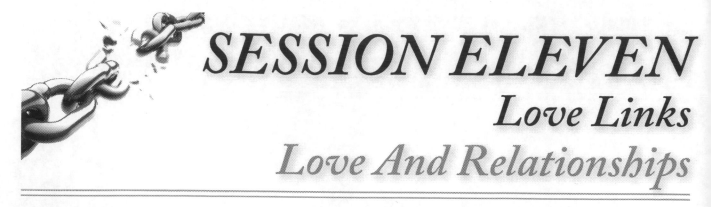

SESSION ELEVEN
Love Links
Love And Relationships

Session Eleven is all about examining our thoughts and beliefs about love, relationships, and issues including commitment, vows, conflict, and what God's Word says about these things.

Most participants will have some very negative thoughts about marriage, and they may be afraid to even consider marriage in their future.

God invented the idea of marriage, and He is clear on how to have a healthy and happy marriage through the good times and the bad. This is a long and very important session, so please be aware of the time.

 ## SESSION GOALS

- Explore your thoughts and attitudes about a loving relationship
- Learn about trust and respect in a healthy marriage
- Reflect on your family patterns and beliefs about vows and commitment
- Learn healthier ways to deal with conflict and confrontations
- Explore what God's Word says about love

 ## GROUP GAB

1. Welcome group members.
2. Go over their session title page (page 76), including the verse.
3. Have participants fill out "All You Need Is Love, Right?" (pages 77-78). Have each person give his or her description of love and marriage.

"Living as one" means full commitment to your spouse's happiness and the strength of your marriage. It also means wanting each other to be the best that God made them to be. Another important part of "living as one" is both of you making your marriage a priority and treating each other the way you would like to be treated.

 ## LINK OF TRUTH: LOVE THAT LASTS A LIFETIME

Do you believe it is possible for you to have a lifelong marriage without divorce? Why or why not? One of the most important things we want you to believe is that just because your parents divorced, it doesn't mean that you are predestined to the same failure. Maybe you have already been unsuccessful at relationships or marriage. Your ideas about love and marriage have no doubt been influenced most by your parents' relationship. You have probably seen good times and you have also seen the failure of their marriage. Maybe the vast amount of marriages you know have been failures and you are now assuming that it isn't possible to have a long-term healthy marriage in our world today.

This may have left you with a fear of commitment or the hope that your marriage will be successful. You may find it difficult to trust or are afraid your spouse will abandon you, so why set yourself up for more hurt and failure.

Sometimes, weddings and the months leading up to it have warning signs that it may not be the best idea. Arguments, control issues and family drama rear their ugly heads, but they ignore them and chalk them up to the stress of the event and realize later that these were warning signs.

If you have been married more than once, there are other issues to explore. We take our baggage from one relationship to another if we don't resolve them and heal from them (baggage such as an unfaithful spouse, financial control, abuse of any kind, abandonment, betrayal, etc.) We come into the next relationship with deep wounds and many times, the new relationship pays for the one we had before. This doesn't set anyone or any relationship up for success.

Each person comes into a new relationship with their own experiences, good or bad and their own expectations as well. Many times, couples don't know enough about each other's journey and so they don't have a chance to work through things and see how they are going to build a healthy relationship. Every marriage is worth taking valuable time to explore each other's past. What are your issues and from where do they originate? Examine your spiritual lives. Are you unified and compatible in this vital area of your relationship? Compare your emotional strengths and weaknesses. How do each of you handle conflict and confrontations? Sexual issues? Financial pressures? What are your values in life? Who have been your role models of marriage and/or commitments which might affect your relationship with each other?

If one or both of you have had parents who have divorced, there are many issues to work through and *Chained No More* can help. Quality Christian counseling is always a good idea.

Marriage, in God's perfect design, was meant to be "until death do us part". When you say those vows, you are saying them to God first and your spouse secondly. It is something to be sure of and then completely commit yourself.

God invented love and marriage. The love He wanted for His children to enjoy is unconditional love—a love that is not selfish, competitive, hurtful, jealous, controlling, or arrogant. His Word is clear that He wants us to enjoy love that includes, joy, humility, selflessness, peace, encouragement, forgiveness, and patience and is full of the fruit of the Spirit. "The fruit of the Spirit is love, joy, peace, patience, kindness, goodness, faithfulness, gentleness and self-control" (Galatians 5:22-23). Now, a marriage based on *those* things will be successful and can last a lifetime!

 # SMALL GROUPS

Have students fill out "Vows, Promises, and Commitment" (pages 79-80) and then discuss their answers. Give them some time to fill out the top portion of "Conflict, Tension, and Confrontation" (page 81) and then go over the bottom portion and pages 81-82 together.

As a large group, go over "Trust and Respect" (pages 83-84). You may have each person, including leaders, read one or a leader might want to read the entire thing aloud. These are important issues to go over, and students may have some things to share about this, so save enough time for that, if possible. Remind them that they will be able to take these books home soon and can use them as resources for years to come.

If you have time, go over "Extra Hints to Keep the Peace" (page 85).

LEADER NOTE: You may not have the time to go over every single page, so you might just give the participants the "Trust and Respect" and "Extra Hints" pages to go over at home, by making extra copies. Strongly encourage them to go over these pages if you don't do it in class. These contain invaluable tools and hints to help them be successful in marriage.

Make sure you have time to go over "Love and God's Word" (page 86). Have participants fill in the spaces. You may cover this page earlier, eliminate something, or extend this session to the next week. Some of this depends on the size of the class, which could determine the amount of time for discussions. Use your best judgment and ask the Lord to guide you in this. This is a very important chapter.

 # PRAYER REQUESTS AND PRAISES

NOTES

MAKING A NEW CHAIN

(Part One)

...ONE LINK AT A TIME

SESSION TWELVE
Making A New Chain (Part One)
Changing Old Patterns

Session Twelve is all about examining our thoughts and behavior patterns and how they affect our lives. This session will also help participants look at how they would like their lives to be different and examine their hopes and dreams.

Many times, we get so caught up on trying to survive day to day that we don't allow ourselves to look into what our future could look like. In doing that, we may miss out on what God has planned for us.

This session could be very enlightening and exciting for students as they look forward with hope and healing. May God bless you as you encourage them to move forward into a much brighter future.

 SESSION GOALS

- Realize your old patterns of thoughts and behavior
- Examine what you were and what you want to become
- Reflect on the influences you have in your life and how they may be affecting you
- Allow yourself to look at your dreams for the future and find a way to achieve them

 GROUP GAB

1. Welcome group members.
2. Have each person tell the most exciting thing he or she has ever done.
3. Go over their session title page (page 88), including the verse.
4. Have participants fill out "What's On Your Mind?" (page 90). When all are done, read the verse at the end of the page out loud as a group.

LINK OF TRUTH: LOOKING IN THE MIRROR

LEADERS: Make sure you have brought an inexpensive mirror (larger than a compact size) for every person (to keep or borrow) so he or she can look at it through the next exercises.

"What do you see when you look in the mirror? Do you see a perfect face—someone with a perfect body? Do you see someone who has it all together, or do you see someone who is flawed? Do you see deep sadness, great joy, or something in between? Do you see someone who has a hurting heart or someone who has received healing from the Lord Jesus?

Do you see only what a human can see, or do you see who God says you are? Do you see years of insecurity or a growing faith and confidence in your standing with Him?

Take some time to look in the mirror you have been given. Look deep, and get real. *That* is the face that Jesus loves. *You* are the person who Jesus forgives, accepts, and will never walk away from."

SOLO TIME

LEADERS: Let the participants find a place to fill out "Looking In the Mirror" (page 90) privately. Pray for them as they fill it out; pray that they will look deeply at how God can change them and what they are willing to do as well.

SMALL GROUPS

Have a variety of markers available.

Have the group fill out "In a Perfect World" (page 91) and share with each other when done. For older participants, you might ask them how they would like to see their life in one to five years.

LINK OF TRUTH: BIG GROUP

What are your hopes and dreams? Maybe you had dreams of being a happy, carefree kid who played sports, sang, went to the movies or a picnic as one happy family. Maybe you had hopes of playing baseball with your dad and growing up to be just like him; a hero in your mind. Maybe you had dreams of being married with the traditional white picket fence with 2.5 children. What happened? Did your dreams come true?

Kids sometimes have to grow up very fast for a variety of reasons. There may have been abuse, a parent with addictions, neglect, or abandonment. You may have tried to live out your parents' hopes for you, by having too many responsibilities or activities. Maybe your parents didn't know how to just let you be a kid of innocence, hopes and dreams. What happened to that little boy/girl you were meant to be?

Many times, as adults, living with shattered hopes and dreams, we get so caught up trying to survive day to day that we don't allow ourselves to look into what our future could look like. In doing that, we may miss out on what God has planned for us. This can be very enlightening and exciting as you look forward with hope and healing.

This session has been about looking forward instead of just looking back. It is, in essence, "looking out of the windshield instead of the rear view mirror". Think about that for a moment. If you were driving a car and all you did was look out the rearview mirror, you would bump into things, run off the road or be fatally injured. If all you did was look out of the windshield and never checked your rear view mirror, you may be hit from behind or not see a potential problem coming up.

The same thing goes for our lives. If we just look at our past and live in its issues, we cannot move forward in safety and strength. If we only look forward but not remember what was before, we could fall back into the same traps and patterns we were in. The past needs to be dealt with, but not completely forgotten. It is part of who we are, but it doesn't have power over us as we "drive away from it".

PRAYER REQUESTS AND PRAISES

NOTES

MAKING A NEW CHAIN
(Part Two)

...ONE LINK AT A TIME

SESSION THIRTEEN
Making A New Chain (Part Two)
Developing New Patterns

Session Thirteen is the last chapter of teaching and working before the big celebration and debrief. This chapter will help participants consider where they need self-improvement and will help them decide what steps they need to take.

SESSION GOALS

· Examine the subject of change—how to truly attain it in areas of your life with God's help and move forward in freedom, *chained no more*

· Reflect on the areas that need to be built up in the future and strategize about how you will make those changes

GROUP GAB

1. Welcome group members.
2. Go over their session title page (page 94), including the verse.
3. Have each person share a couple of changes he or she has made in his or her life for the better and how he or she did it.

LINK OF TRUTH: TAKING STEPS INTO A HEALTHIER AND HAPPIER FUTURE

How comfortable are you with changes in your life? Is it difficult for you to adjust to change or do you embrace change and make the necessary adjustments?

Life changes can feel like a train whizzing by while you stand beside the track. It can almost knock you over and make you unsteady for a long period of time. Sometimes, however, you barely notice changes at all.

You may find yourself in a dark place at the present time and you see no way out. Maybe there is nothing you can do to change your circumstances, but God can help you change your perspective and make the most of where you are. Seem impossible? Nothing is impossible with God and His plan. There is hope for you and a better future ahead.

You have the opportunity to begin to structure your life on many levels—personally, relationally, spiritually, etc. This may be the ending of this class, but it is just the beginning for you.

Hopefully you can stop defining yourself by your past now and look forward to what and who will define you from this moment on. God's Word is full of statements about who you are and about His plan and purpose for you. Let God be your guiding light in this journey. Now, let's work on how you are going to rebuild your life. Go over "Change" (page 95) and discuss. This page is vital.

SMALL GROUPS

LEADERS: Have students work on "Rebuilding Your Life" and the accompanying work pages (pages 96-98).

Bring the class back together, and congratulate the participants for the hard work they have put into this journey of *Chained No More*. Thank them for their openness and their encouragement of others.

Have each person fill out "Links Learned" (page 99), and let them share their answers with the class. This should be very encouraging to all.

Let participants know your leaders will continue to pray for them and that if they need to talk, they can connect with you. Make sure they have your contact information, if you want them to have it.

Encourage participants to be consistent in going to church and plugging in as well as spending time reading God's Word and talking to Him. *This* is what their lives need to be based on, not their past, society, or what others think. Let God's truth be your truth! Please go over "Putting Feet to Your Prayers" (page 100) and maybe give examples of your own.

LINK OF TRUTH

Rebuilding anything takes a plan, active steps, time and patience. This is your life and rebuilding it will take all of these components we have learned in this session. One step at a time. Ask God to show you the way. He will, because He wants you to be whole again and live a life of joy, freedom and strength in Him. Each day is another day of living "chained no more". May God bless you as you continue your journey. If you find areas that trip you up, please be willing to find a good counselor, pastor, therapist, or chaplain to help you take more steps toward healing. You can also go back through this book and review to help you get back on track.

LEADERS: If you can, it would be a good idea to put together a resource page of quality Christian counselors, therapists, pastors, etc. for your participants to contact after completing this program, if they need to.

PRAYER REQUESTS AND PRAISES

You might hand out the list of prayer requests and praises that you shared throughout the thirteen weeks. This can build faith in God's faithfulness and provision.

PLEASE REMIND THE CLASS THAT THE NEXT WEEK'S CLASS WILL BE AN EVENING OF CELEBRATION AND DEBRIEFING. TELL CLASS MEMBERS TO COME READY TO ENJOY A FUN TIME TOGETHER.

NOTES

CHAINED NO MORE

CELEBRATION

SESSION FOURTEEN
Chained No More
Celebration

Session Fourteen is all about celebrating what the Lord has done and the healing that has happened in the lives of your students. You probably see immense healing and improvement in them, and your heart is blessed beyond words at what God has done!

From the moment the participants walk in, let the atmosphere be light and celebratory, because they have earned it. Here are some suggestions:

- Have fun music playing.
- Serve something special for dinner.
- Play charades, Catch Phrase, Apples to Apples, or another big group game.
- Give participants meaningful gifts, such as a Bible that all leaders and your pastor signed, a flower for each person, or a pen and an encouraging note from each leader that describes what you have seen in them.
- **NOTE:** Another exceptional idea is to purchase *"A Mind Renewed by God"*, by Dr. Kimball Hodge for each participant. This book will continue them on their way to a much brighter and stronger future. You can order them by going to kimlyndahodge@gmail.com.

Be creative in how you run this evening and have fun!

Make sure you give the participants plenty of time to fill out the "Chained No More Debrief Form," in the Participant Book, make a copy and send it to our office or e-mail comments to us so we can continue to improve this program for future groups. Ask each person to explain one thing that he or she learned in this class that has made a difference in his or her thinking, beliefs or actions.

✳ PRAYER REQUESTS AND PRAISES

During this last time of prayer together, hand out sheets of paper so each person can write down the others' requests. Then ask the participants to commit to praying for each other in the future.

You might offer to have a social reconnect in a month or two and plan that event. Make sure you have everyone's contact information before the night is over. Please set up healthy boundaries with the participants who have just completed the class. Some will "hang on" and still want to connect with you in strong ways. Pray for wisdom in this area.

Well done, leaders! We have been praying for
all of you each week and would welcome your
suggestions and/or concerns.
Send feedback to

robyn@robynbministries.com

APPENDIX

SMALL GROUPS
The Whys And Whats
By Robyn Besemann

Small group time can be a very effective tool to connect with group members in a much deeper way. It allows time to step away from the large group, reflect on important issues and allow leaders to minister on a deeper level.

There can be some challenges in these groups that can effect the outcome including:

CHALLENGE: The person who seems to monopolize the time with his or her story and issues

ISSUES: This person may be buried in crisis and sharing for the first time.
This person may have isolated himself or herself up until the present time and need to talk.
This person may be completely focused on himself or herself only.

WHAT TO DO: Begin the group by asking everyone to be considerate about not monopolizing the small group time. If anyone needs to talk longer, he or she can talk with a leader after the class or during the week. Remind participants of this during the small group time, if necessary. Be sensitive to others in the group by gently ending a long-winded response.

CHALLENGE: The person who uses inappropriate language or explicit information

ISSUES: This person may have a habit of bad language.
This person may like to shock people.
This person may think it is funny to do this to rebel in a church.
This person may be disrespecting you as a leader.
This person may be trying to show that he or she has the worst story.

WHAT TO DO: Remind them about not using inappropriate language. Explain that it is important not to offend one another and be sensitive. If you need to, have a leader take this person aside to talk about it.

CHALLENGE: The person who doesn't participate

ISSUES: This person may just naturally be shy.
This person may have been abused and is shut down.
This person may not be ready to open up yet because trust hasn't been built.
This person may be feeling intimidated and is afraid of rejection.

WHAT TO DO: Approach this person gently until trust can be built.
Acknowledge the individual throughout the small group.
Do not beg him or her or insist that he or she share. Let the person share when he or she is ready. Do not intimidate or ridicule the person, and don't let other group members, either. The group should be a safe place. Encourage them to answer a light or general question first.

CHALLENGE: The person who seems to want to be the leader, give advice, and try to run the group

ISSUES: This person may find it easier to look at others' issues than his or her own.
This person may be looking for ways to feel important about himself or herself and what he or she knows.
This person may like to be in control of all situations.

WHAT TO DO: Remind the person that you need to ask the questions. Remind him or her that if we focus only on others, we will miss the journey that God has for us personally. Let the individual know, however, that if he or she has concerns about the small group, he or she can come and talk to you about it after the class that night.

To begin small groups successfully, please give your group the following guidelines:

- Everyone is important and should have the opportunity to share. Try not to monopolize the time.
- If anyone wants to share more, then encourage him or her to talk with you after the class or during the week.
- You are the leader and will try to be sensitive to everyone within the time constraints.
- Sometimes it is easier to focus on other people and their issues than on your own
- This is a time for participants to look deeper and build a stronger trust and bond with those in your group.
- The small groups are for participants to explore their issues and head toward healing, so please don't feel that you, as a leader, need to do more talking than they do. Listen much more than you speak, and let the Holy Spirit guide you in what to do and say.
- If an issue comes up during the small group that you don't know how to address, don't try to fake an answer, but keep silent or tell the person you will look into it and get back to him or her next week. Make sure you do that so the participants can learn to trust your word.
- Make sure you share your small group experience with the other leaders at the end of the session so you are all on the same page and can minister more effectively as a team.

CREDITS AND RESOURCES

CONTRIBUTORS:

Dr. Kimball Hodge III, D.Min., pastor and author (kimlyndahodge@gmail.com)—Central Point, Oregon

Dr. Marlin Schultz, D.Min., marriage/family therapist—Eugene, Oregon

Linda Ranson-Jacobs, speaker, writer, and developer of *Divorce Care for Kids (hlp4.com)*
—Navarre, Florida

Elsa Colopy, speaker and author (www.elsakokcolopy.com)—Colorado Springs, Colorado

Krista Smith, developer of *The Big D...Divorce Thru the Eyes of a Teen*—(sonsetpointministries.com)

Pastor Colin Halstead, MA therapist, pastor of Renewal Ministries at Eugene
First Baptist Church (colinh@fbceugene.com)—Eugene, Oregon

Many people interviewed who are adult children of divorce and were willing to share their stories
and the many effects that their parents' divorces had on their lives

Most importantly, the Lord God; His guidance in writing this material
is the best contribution of all

RESOURCE MATERIALS:

The Bible—God's Word

Between Two Worlds by Elizabeth Marquardt, Three Rivers Press, 2005

A Mind Renewed by God by Dr. Kimball Hodge III, Harvest House Publishers, 1998
(kimlyndahodge@gmail.com)

The Big D...Divorce Thru the Eyes of a Teen, by Krista Smith, AMFM Press, 2010
(sonsetpointministries.com)

Divorce Care for Kids (DC4K) by Linda Ranson-Jacobs, Church Initiative, 2004 (hlp4.com)

Adult Children of Divorce by Jim Conway InterVarsity Press, 1990

"The Telemark Age", cartoon by Alan d'Egville. Courtesy of the Ski Club of Great Britain